Snow Day

Written by Howard Wells
Photographs by John Paul Endress

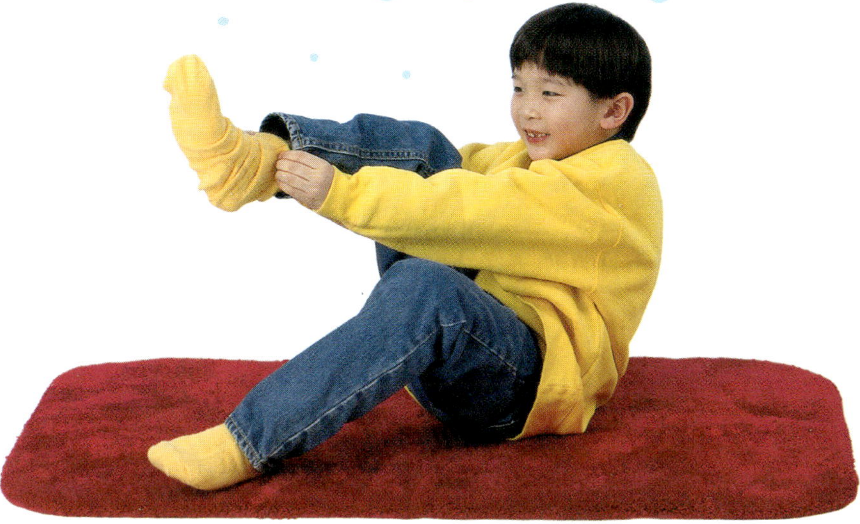

Celebration Press
Parsippany, New Jersey

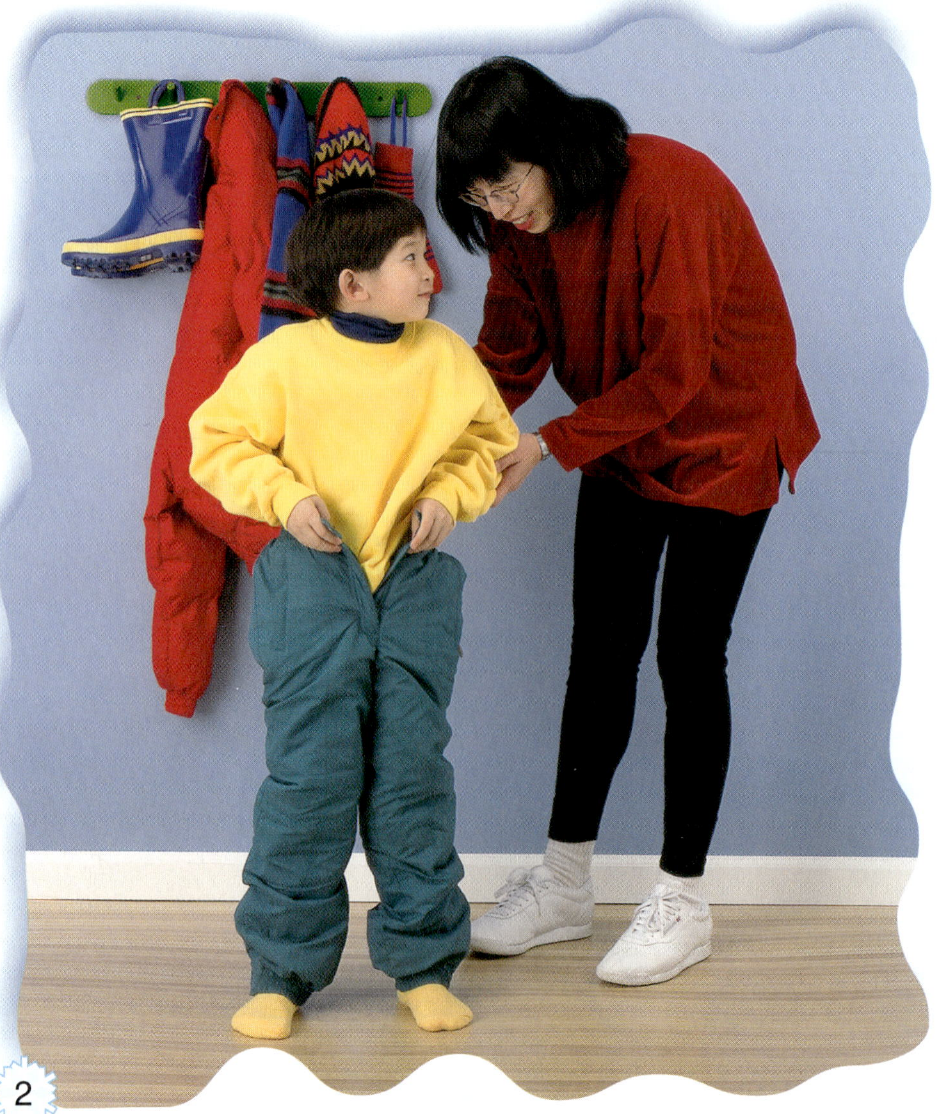

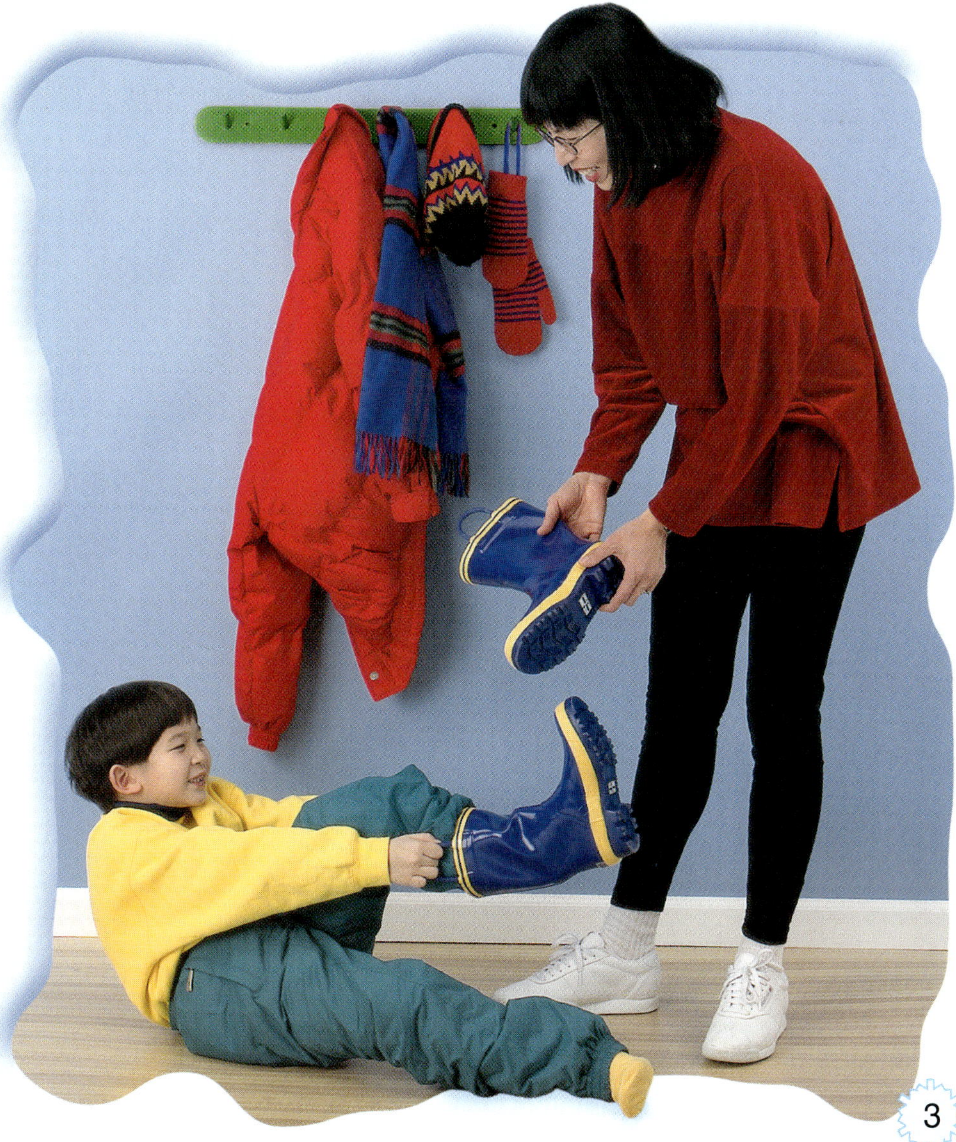

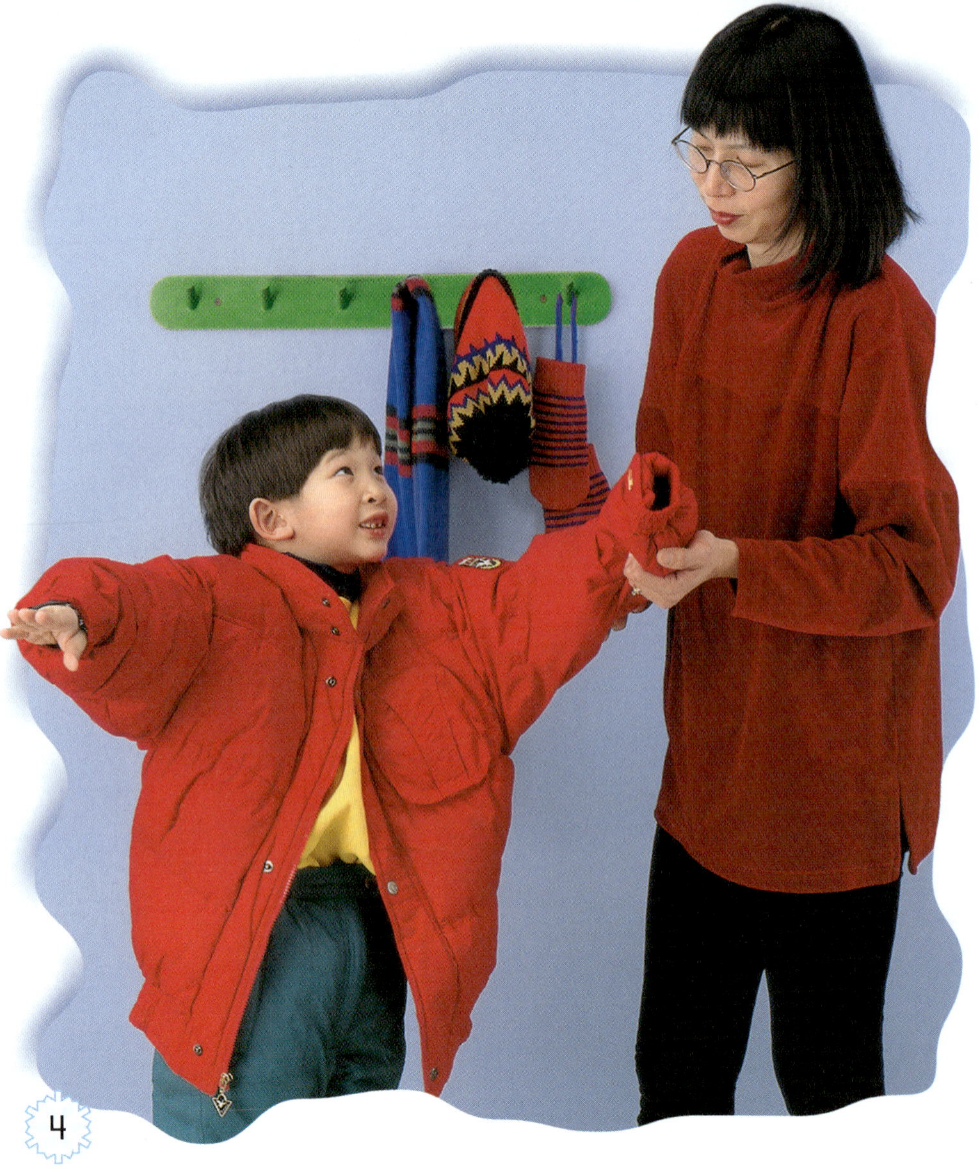

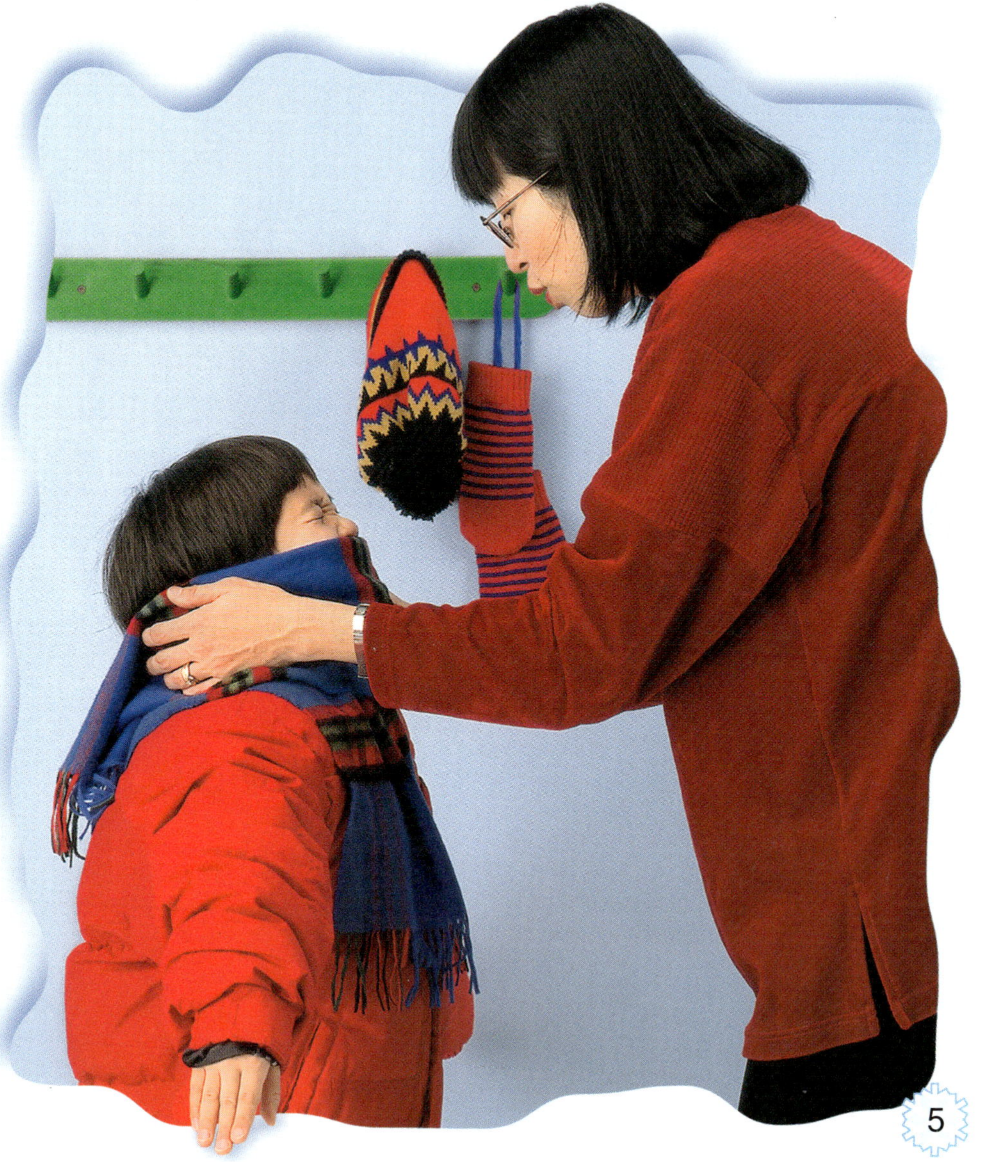

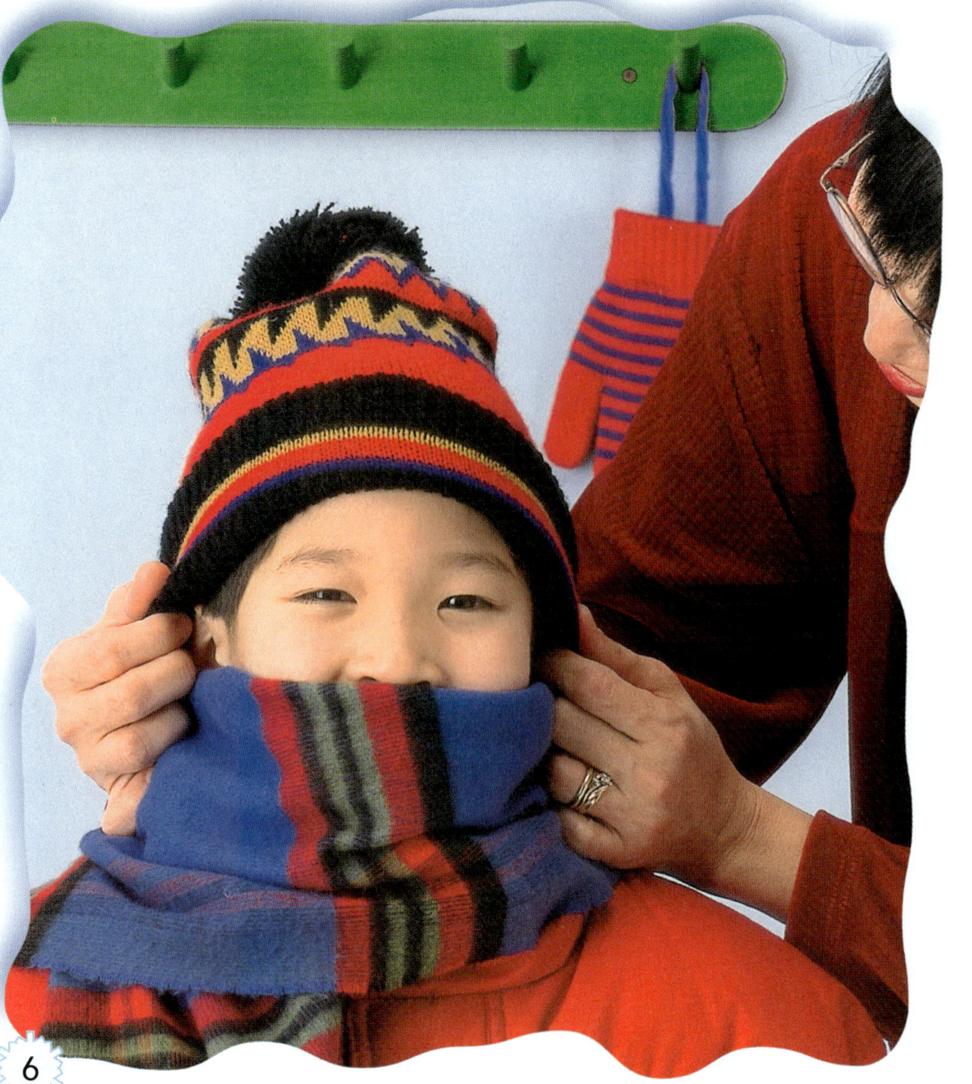

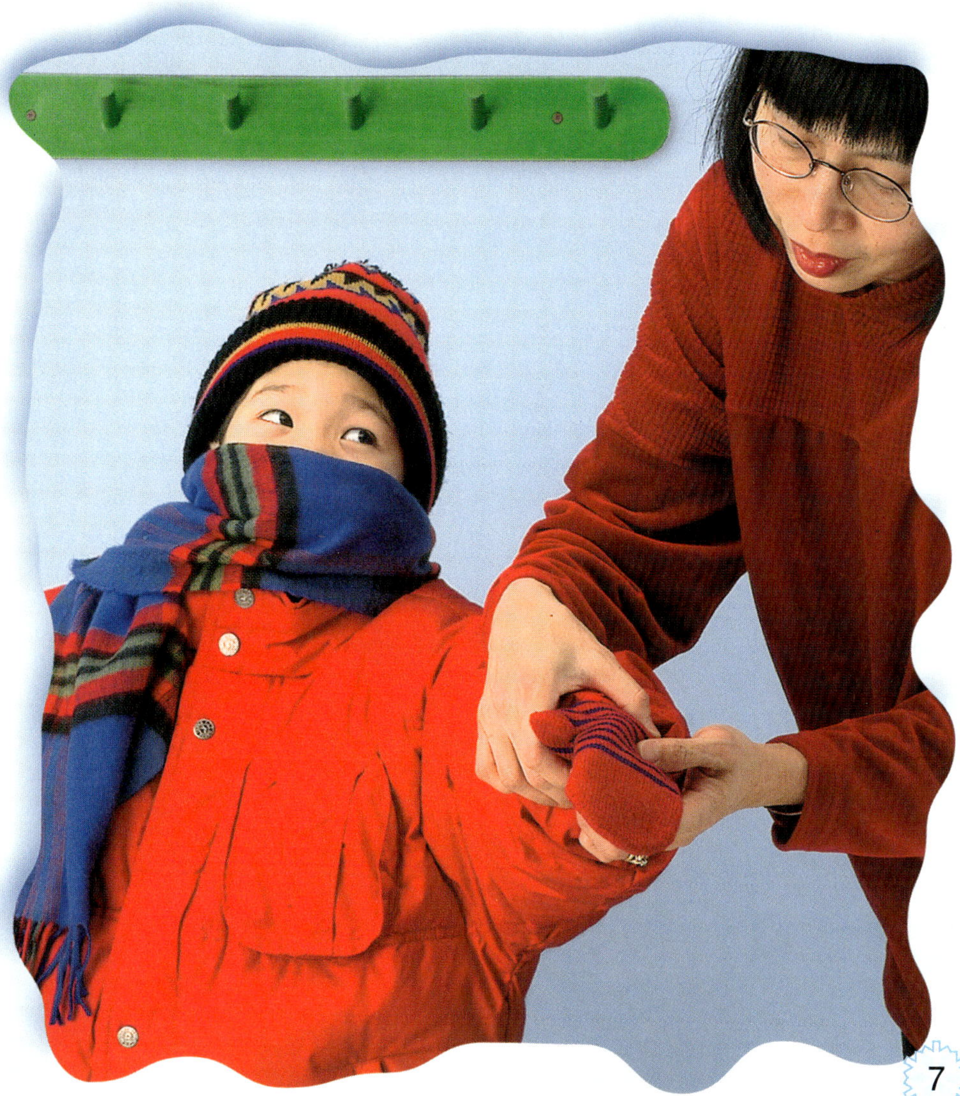

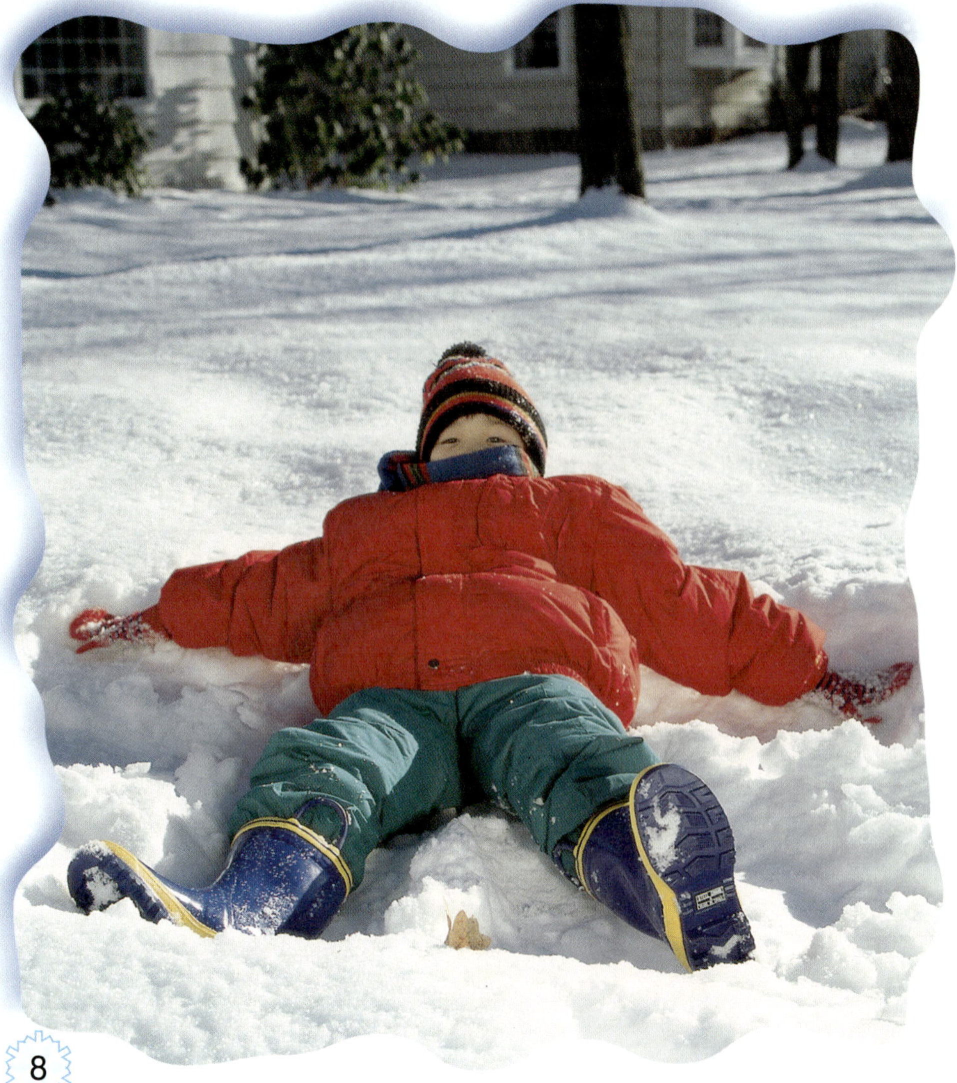